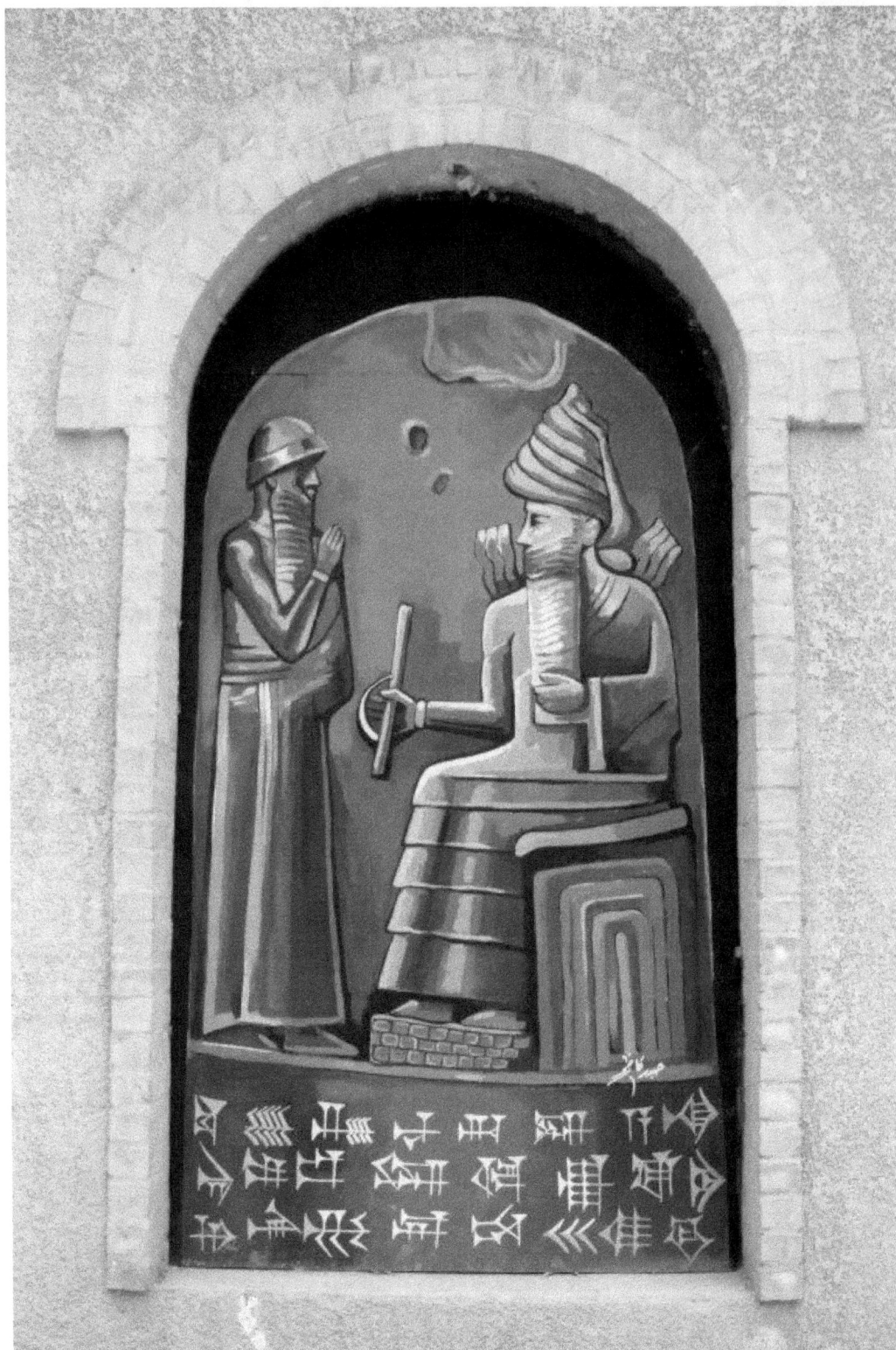

Code of Hammurabi

READ AND WRITE
MODERN ARAMAIC
IN CHALDEAN DIALOGUE
BY
FR. MICHAEL J. BAZZI
PASTOR Emeritus OF
ST. PETER CHALDEAN
CATHOLIC CATHEDRAL

Published by:
Let in the Light Publishing
letinthelightpublishing@gmail.com
www.letinthelightpublishing.com

Copyright, 2017 by Michael J. Bazzi
ISBN: 978-1-941464-04-5

Formatting and layout by Kheloud Issa Allos
Cover Photo Credit: Bernadit Seman. Ishtar Gate. Babylon, Iraq.

Introduction

The purpose of this study is to introduce Modern Aramaic-Chaldean Dialect to a new generation of Chaldeans and all those who have a desire to read, write, and converse in it. Language is the most precious heritage we possess. I feel it is a great honor for me to be able to provide this simple method for learning Aramaic — the language of Jesus and His disciples, and to share in the new revival movement of this famous and ancient language.

Today, there are literally millions of Chaldeans, Assyrians, and Syrians throughout the world who use Aramaic in their own dialect in their daily living. The task of keeping this most valuable treasure alive is a responsibility that belongs to all of us.

A Brief History of the Chaldeans

The Chaldeans are originally from the great country of Mesopotamia, also known as ''The Cradle of Civilization.'' Today this ancient country is known as Iraq. The age-old scattered tribes of the Chaldeans lived among the lakes and swamp that bordered the middle and lower courses of the Tigris and Euphrates rivers from Babylon to the Sea of Chaldea, lately known as the Persian or Arabian Gulf. Industrious Chaldeans became well-known scientists, merchants, farmers, ranchers and herdsmen who transformed the world through their understanding of astronomy, mathematics, numerology, and numerous other sciences. The mighty Chaldean warriors established the famous Babylonian Empire, whose frontiers extended from Mesopotamia to Syria between 626 and 539 BC Palestine, Lebanon, Arabia and Egypt (the Bible confirms this history especially in the books of Kings, Chronicles and the Prophets).

Six Chaldean kings ruled this vast empire in succession. King Nebuchadnezzar II was the second ruling monarch of the Chaldean nation (605-562 BC). He made the city of Babylon one of the most magnificent cities of that time by erecting the famous ''hanging gardens,'' one of the seven wonders of the ancient world. He beautified the city by building rose-colored walls, wide processional streets, blue-glazed bricks decorated with red- dragons, lions and wild bulls, canals, artificial lakes, and a large reservoir that surrounded Babylon. Though the Chaldean empire succumbed to Persian rule in 538 BC, its people remained indomitable and flourished throughout history to the present day.

The Chaldeans were converted to Christianity by the ministry of St. Thomas the Apostle and Mar Addai and Mar Mari in the first century AD. Shortly after their conversion, Chaldeans established the Church of the East. By the end of the fifth century AD, the Church of the East separated from the Church of Rome. During this period, the Chaldean Church prospered and expanded throughout Chaldea, Assyria, Iran, Arabia, Mongolia, China, and in Malabar, India.

In 1445 AD and 1553 AD, a large portion of the Chaldean church was reunited with the Church of Rome in India. At the end of the nineteenth century, there were two million Christians who adhered to the hierarchy of the Church of the East in Mesopotamia and used the Aramaic language for their liturgy.

A Brief History of the Aramaic Language

The Aramaic language made its historical appearance sometime between the sixteenth and the fourteenth centuries BC in Mesopotamia and its alphabet became the vehicle for communication all over the Near East. It gradually supplanted other tongues in neighboring lands. Between the years 1077 and 911 BC, the nomadic Aramaen tribes had conquered Babylon and ruled over parts of Mesopotamia. Throughout this period Aramaic became the commercial language and from the ninth century to the seventh century BC The Aramaic language itself went through many stages of development:

Old Aramaic	**925-700 BC**
Standard Aramaic	**700-200 BC**
Middle Aramaic	**200 BC-200 AD**
Late Aramaic	**200 AD-700 AD**

Some scholars estimate that in the sixth century AD the Aramaic language began to fragment regionally into Eastern and Western. The Western Aramaic language became the dialect of the Jews and the Syriac form. Eastern Aramaic was the dialect spoken of Chaldean and Assyrian form, Talmudic Aramaic, and Mundaien. Modern Aramaic is considered to have begun around 700 AD and is still spoken today.

Mesopotamians had adopted Aramaic since the tenth century BC and Aramaic became the lingua franca (common language) of the Near East. The Chaldean Empire, beginning in 612 BC carried this Semitic tongue throughout every province and country from Asia Minor in the north to the Arabian Peninsula in the south, and from Egypt in the west to Pakistan in the east. At this time, the language of the people of Palestine shifted from Hebrew to Aramaic because of the influence of the invaders; it continued until the sixth century AD.

After the fall of the Chaldean empire, the Persian nation ruled Mesopotamia and its surrounding area and continued to promulgate the Aramaic language in every facet of life. Thus, when Christianity began to spread from Antioch in Syria to many near Eastern countries, Aramaic became the liturgical language of Christians in Mesopotamia, Iran, Turkey, Armenia, Syria, and Lebanon. It was kept alive domestically and also scholastically.

Classical Aramaic gradually mixed with local languages and, because of the influences of other languages, there are differences in the spoken form of modern Aramaic between countries, regions, and sometimes the neighboring cities and villages. Classical Aramaic is currently used only in its liturgical form and in biblical and historical studies. However, modern Aramaic in its many dialects still remains faithful to its roots.

Fr. Michael Bazzi

April 2017

Contents

Titles by Let in the Light Publishing:

Aramaic Language Chaldean Dialect

Beginner's Handbook of the Aramaic Chaldean Alphabets

Advanced Handbook of Modern Aramaic Language ChaldeanVol. II

Chaldean Nation (English / Arabic)

Chaldeans Past and Present

Classical Aramaic I

Classical Aramaic II

A High School Tennis Coach's Handbook: For Parents, Players, & Coaches

The Life of Tilkepnaye (Paperback Trilingual / Hardback English)

Preserving the Chaldean Aramaic Language

Read and Write the Modern Aramaic in Chaldean Dialect

For more information, or to purchase, please visit our website:

www.letinthelightpublishing.com

Chapter One : ܦܝܩܝܕܐ

Grammar ܗܘܦܝ ܡܡܠܠܐ

The 22 letters (consonants)

of the Aramaic-Chaldean Alphabet:

1st: The 22 Aramaic-Chaldean alphabet

ܝܡܩܒܝ ܘܟܕܩܡܝ ܢܩܦܦܐ ܦܟܬܢܐ ܢܐܬܟܐ - ܟܠܟܢܐ

ܐ ܒ ܓ ܕ ܗ ܘ ܙ ܚ ܛ ܝ ܟ ܠ ܡ ܢ ܣ ܥ ܦ ܨ ܩ ܪ ܫ ܬ

These letters are written and read from right to left. They are divided into six groups:

1-ABGaD 2-HaWaZ 3-H̲aTI 4-KuLMaN 5- SaAPaS̲ 6- QaRSHat

1-	ABGaD	A- ܐ	B- ܒ	G- ܓ	D- ܕ	ܐܒܓܕ	(4 Letters)
2-	HaWaZ	H- ܗ	W- ܘ	Z- ܙ		ܗܘܙ	(3 Letters)
3-	H̲aTY	H̲- ܚ	T̲- ܛ	Y- ܝ		ܚܛܝ	(3 Letters)
4-	KuLMaN	K- ܟ	L- ܠ	M- ܡ	N- ܢ	ܟܠܡܢ	(4 Letters)
5-	SaAPaS̲	S- ܣ	A̲- ܥ	P- ܦ	S̲- ܨ	ܣܥܦܨ	(4 Letters)
6-	QaRSHaT	Q- ܩ	R- ܪ	SH- ܫ	T- ܬ	ܩܪܫܬ	(4 Letters)

2nd: Symbols added over Aramaic letters ܣܡܩܬܐ

ܕܡܘܣܦܝ : ܠܟܬܐ

- Out of the 22 letters of the Aramaic alphabet the following five letters have no precise equivalent in English, they are indicated with a small line beneath the letter. In the following chart for the sake of the Arabic learner, the Arabic letters are written in the middle of each, for example:

1		2		3		4		5	
ܚ	ح **H̲**	ܛ	ط **T̲**	ܥ	ع **A̲**	ܨ	ص **S̲**	ܩ	ق **Q**

Note: See page 9 for other symbols

3rd : The names, sizes & styles of the Aramaic alphabet

	Name	Eng	Aram	Size/Writing	Steps in Aramaic	Name	#
1-	Alap	A	ܐ	Size 3 over the base line		ܐܠܦ	1
2-	Beth	B	ܒ	Size 2 over the base line		ܒܝܬ	2
3-	Gamal	G	ܓ	Size 3 over the base line & size 1 below line base		ܓܡܠ	3
4-	Dalath	D	ܕ	Size 2 over the base line & short horizontal line below		ܕܠܬ	4
5-	He	H	ܗ	Size 2 over the base line		ܗܐ	5
6-	Wow	O	ܘ	Size 2 over the base line		ܘܘ	6
7-	Zayn	Z	ܙ	Size 2 over the base line- size 1 below		ܙܝܢ	7
8-	Heth	H̱	ܚ	Size 1 over the base line		ܚܝܬ	8
9-	Teth	T̲	ܛ	Size 3 over the base line- 2 below		ܛܝܬ	9
10-	Yod	E, I, Y	ܝ	Size 1 over the base line		ܝܘܕ	10
11-	Kap w Kap	C K	ܟ	Size 2 over the base line		ܟܦ ܘܟܦ	20
12-	Lamad	L	ܠ	Size 4 over the base line		ܠܡܕ	30
13-	Meem w Meem	M	ܡ	Size 2 over the base line		ܡܝܡ	40
				The Final M		ܘܡܝܡ	
14-	Noon w Noon	N	ܢ	Size 2 over the base line		ܢܘܢ	50
15-	Simkath	S	ܣ	Size 2 over the base line		ܣܡܟܬ	60
16	Ae	A̲	ܥ	Size 3 over the base line		ܥܐ	70
17-	Pe	P	ܦ	Size 3 over the base line		ܦܐ	80
18-	Sade	S̲	ܨ	Size 1 over the base line- 2 below		ܨܕܐ	90
19-	Qop	Q	ܩ	Size 2 over the base line		ܩܘܦ	100
20-	Resh	R	ܪ	Size 2 over the base line Short horizontal line above		ܪܝܫ	200
21-	Sheen	Sh	ܫ	Size 2 over the base line		ܫܝܢ	300
22-	Taw w taw	T	ܬ	Size 3 over the base line		ܬܘ ܘ ܬܘ	400

4th : The 26 English alphabet, with the equivalent Aramaic alphabet and sounds

A	ܐ	B	ܒ	C	ܟ	D	ܕ	E	ܗ	F-sound	ܦ	G	ܓ
H	ܗ	I	ܝ	J-sound	ܓ	K	ܟ	L	ܠ	M	ܡ	N	ܢ
O-vowel	ܘ	P	ܦ	Q	ܩ	R	ܪ	S	ܣ	T	ܬ	U-vowel	ܘ
V-sound	ܒ	W	ܘ	X	ܟܣ	Y	ܝ	Z	ܙ				

5th: The seven Aramaic vowels ܙܘܥܐ : ܫܒܥܐ : ܩܕܡܝܐ

1	SQAPA- ܙܩܦܐ ܿ	Long A= Aa ܵ example: ܡܵܪܵܐ -(Mara) Lord
2	PTHAHA - ܦܬܚܐ ܲ	Short A= Ah ܲ example: ܡܲܠܟܵܐ -(Malka) King
3	ZLAMA PSHEEQA- ܙܠܵܡܵܐ ܦܫܝܼܩܵܐ ܹ	Short I= I ܼ example: ܡܸܫܚܵܐ -(Mishha) Oil
4	ZLAMA QASHYA- ܙܠܵܡܵܐ ܩܲܫܝܵܐ ܹ	Long E = AY ܹ example: ܪܹܫܵܐ -(Raysha) Head
5	RWAHA - ܪܘܵܚܵܐ ܿ	Long O=OH ܿ example: ܦܘܿܩܵܐ -(Poqa) Nose
6	RWASA - ܪܘܵܨܵܐ ܘ	Long U= U ܘ example: ܙܘܼܙܵܐ -(Zooza) Money
7	HWASA - ܚܘܵܨܵܐ ܝ	Long Y- EE ܝ example: ܡܝܼܟܵܐܝܠ -(Mikhael) Michael

Long Y   Long O   Short A   Long E   Long U   Long A Short I

ܠܸܒܵܐ ܡܠܹܐ ܣܘܼܬܵܐ ܠܝܼܕܵܥ ܕܡܵܪܝ ܦܹܛܪܘܿܣ ܫܠܝܼܚܵܐ

(A heart filled with love for St. Peter the Apostle)

3

6th:Transliteration of the 22 alphabet letters

	Letters			Examples				Letters			Examples		
1-	Alap	A	ܐ	August	AB	ܐܒ	12-	Lama<u>d</u>	L	ܠ	Heart	libba	ܠܒܐ
2-	Beth	B	ܒ	Father	Baba	ܒܒܐ	13-	Meem	M	ܡ	King	Malka	ܡܠܟܐ
3-	Gamal	G	ܓ	Fortune	Bone	ܓܪܡܐ	14-	Noon	N	ܢ	Noah	No<u>h</u>	ܢܘܚ
4-	Dalath	D	ܕ	Bear	Dibba	ܕܒܐ	15-	Simkath	S	ܣ	Horse	Soos	ܣܘܣ
5-	He	H	ܗ	One time	Gaha	ܓܗܐ	16-	<u>Ae</u>	A	ܥ	World	<u>A</u>-alma	ܥܠܡܐ
6-	Waw	W, O, U	ܘ	Goose	Wazza	ܘܙܐ	17-	Pe	P	ܦ	Half	Palga	ܦܠܓܐ
7-	Zayn	Z	ܙ	Money	Zooza	ܙܘܙܐ	18-	<u>S</u>ade	<u>S</u>	ܨ	Fast	<u>S</u>awma	ܨܘܡܐ
8-	<u>H</u>eth	<u>H</u>	ܚ	Eve	<u>H</u>awa	ܚܘܐ	19-	Qop	Q	ܩ	Pencil	Qalama	ܩܠܡܐ
9-	<u>T</u>eth	<u>T</u>	ܛ	Deer	<u>T</u>oya	ܛܒܝܐ	20-	Resh	R	ܪ	Great	Raba	ܪܒܐ
10-	Yo<u>d</u>	E, I, Y	ܝ	Mother	Yimma	ܝܡܐ	21-	Sheen	Sh	ܫ	Name	Shemma	ܫܡܐ
11-	Kap	K, C, Q	ܟ	Tooth	Kaka	ܟܟܐ	22-	Taw	T	ܬ	Snow	Talga	ܬܠܓܐ

7th: The three Aramaic letters (K, M, N) that have different final form

1- K- Kap (ܟ)

  a. Initial K (ܟ), for example (ܟܠܕܝܐ) Chaldean

  b. Medial K (ܟ), for example (ܡܠܟܐ) king

  c. Final K for joining letter (ܟ ـ), for example (ܒܥܠܒܟ) (Ba-alabak) the city of Biblos.

d. Final K for enjoining letter (ܟ) for example (ܟܪܟܘܟ) (Karkuk) the city of Karkuk.

2. M-Meem (ܡ)

a- Initial M (ܡ), for example (ܡܪܩܘܣ) (Marqus) Mark

b- Medial M (ـܡـ), for example (ܥܠܡܐ) (Aalma) the world

Final M after both joining and enjoining letter is (ܡ) for example (ܡܪܝܡ) (Mariam) Mary

3. N- Noon (ܢ)

a- Initial N (ܢ), for example (ܢܘܪܐ) (Noora) fire

b- Medial N (ـܢـ), for example (ܚܢܢܐ) (Hnana) mercy

c- Final N after joining letter (ܢ), for example (ܝܘܚܢܢ) (Yuhanan) John

d- Final N after enjoining letter (ܢ), for example (ܫܡܥܘܢ) (Shim-aon) Simon.

When reciting the 22 letters of the alphabet, these letters (K, M, N) have two forms, and both forms are mensioned.

1. K kap w kap (ܟܝ) (ܟܦ ܘܟܦ)

2. M meem w meem (ܡܝܡ) (ܡܝܡ ܘܡܝܡ)

3. N noon w noon (ܢ) (ܢܘܢ ܘܢܘܢ)

8th: Extra notes

- There are nine **sounds; four** of them have no precise equivalent English letters. (GHܓ / D ܕ / KH ـܟ /Dh ܝ) While the rest have equivalent English letters (Jܓ /CH ـܟ /F ܦ /V ܦ /TH ܬ).

- Some writers use different symbol for **f** ܦ pronounced as **fa** And for **dh** ܨ pronounced as **dha**.

- The five Aramaic letters and four sounds that do not exist in English, have been marked with either a **small line or one thick dot or three thick dots or small upside down v** beneath the letter-sound or over it or **combination of two letters**, as it shows in the following nine sounds that have no precise equivalent English letters:

1	2	3	4	5	6	7	8	9
ܓ ܔ Gh	ܕ ذ D	خ ـܟ: KH	ܦ ق V	ض ظ ܘ Dh	ܓ ج J	ج ـܟ CH	ܦ ف F	ܬ ث TH

9th: The plural points ܗܢܩܕ

A plural noun is indicated by placing two small horizontal dashes above one of its letters. These dashes are called the plural points.

Singular			plural		
King	ܡܲܠܟܵܐ	Malka	Kings	ܡܲܠܟܹܐ	Malke
Country	ܐܲܬܪܵܐ	Athra	Countries	ܐܲܬܪܵܘܵܬ݂ܵܐ	Athrawatha
Cold	ܩܲܪܝܼܪܵܐ	Qareera	Colds	ܩܲܪܝܼܪܹܐ	Qareere

10th: There are four distinguished sizes for writing the Aramaic alphabet

Size One

	1	2	3
Letters	Heth	Yod	Sade
	H	E,I,Y	S
	ܚ	ܝ	ܨ
	Eve	John	Fast
Example	ܚܵܘܵܐ	ܝܘܿܚܲܢܢ	ܨܲܘܡܵܐ

Size Two

	1	2	3	4	5	6	7	8	9	10	11	12
Letters	Beth	Dalath	He	Waw	Zayn	Kap	Meem	Noon	Simkath	Qop	Resh	Sheen
	B	D	H	W,O,U	Z	K	M	N	S	Q	R	Sh
	ܒ	ܕ	ܗ	ܘ	ܙ	ܟ	ܡ	ܢ	ܣ	ܩ	ܪ	ܫ
	Human	Bear	Mind	Flower	Money	Karkuk	Mary	Jona	Horse	Sacrifice	Head	Peace
Example	ܒܲܪܢܵܫܵܐ	ܕܸܒܵܐ	ܗܵܘܢܵܐ	ܘܲܪܕܵܐ	ܙܘܿܙܹܐ	ܟܲܪܟܘܼܟ݂	ܡܲܪܝܲܡ	ܢܘܿܢܵܐ	ܣܘܼܣܵܐ	ܩܘܼܪܒܵܢܵܐ	ܪܹܫܵܐ	ܫܠܵܡܵܐ

Size Three

	1	2	3	4	5	6
Letters	Alap	Gamal	Teth	Ae	Pe	Taw
	A	G	T	A	P	T
	ܐ	ܓ	ܛ	ܥ	ܦ	ܬ
	Andrew	Camel	Child	Eye	Savior	Jar
ample	ܐܲܢܕܪܵܘܘܿܣ	ܓܲܡܠܵܐ	ܛܲܠܝܵܐ	ܥܲܝܢܵܐ	ܦܵܪܘܿܩܵܐ	ܚܲܒ݂ܵܐ

Size Four

	1
Letters	Lamad
	L
	ܠ
	Heart
Example	ܠܸܒܵܐ

11th: The Joining and Enjoining of the Aramaic letters

The following chart indicates the six original letters and their modification in script and sound:

A- There are 8 enjoining letters: Each of the 22 alphabet stands unattached from the left side when it is preceded by one of these 8 enjoining letters.

8	7	6	5	4	3	2	1
ܬ	ܪ	ܨ	ܙ	ܗ	ܘ	ܕ	ܐ
ܬܠܡܐ	ܪܡܫܐ	ܨܕܪܐ	ܙܘܡܪܬܐ	ܗܘܢܐ	ܘܙܐ	ܕܝܢܐ	ܐܝܠܢܐ
Jar	Evening	Chest	Song	Mind	Goose	Judgment	Tree

B -There are 14 joining letters: each of these is attached from both sides when it is joined by one of the 22 alphabet.

14	13	12	11	10	9	8	7	6	5	4	3	2	1
ܫ	ܩ	ܦ	ܥ	ܣ	ܢ	ܡ	ܠ	ܟ	ܝ	ܛ	ܚ	ܓ	ܒ
ܫܡܥܐ	ܩܕܝܫܐ	ܦܛܪܘܣ	ܥܡܐ	ܣܡܐ	ܢܘܪܐ	ܡܪܐ	ܠܠܝܐ	ܟܠܕܝܐ	ܝܘܡܐ	ܛܝܪܐ	ܚܠܡܐ	ܓܪܡܐ	ܒܒܠ
Candle	**Saint**	**Peter**	**Uncle**	**Wart**	**Fire**	**Lord**	**Night**	**Chaldean**	**Day**	**Bird**	**Dream**	**Bone**	**Babylon**

12th: The six sounds used in Classical and Modern Aramaic

Because of the influence of neighboring languages, six of the 22 letters were modified in sound in classical Aramaic BGaDiKPaT (ܒ ܓ ܕ ܟ ܦ ܬ) and were added to the alphabet. However, only four of the six letters (ܒ ܟ ܕ ܬ) were given new sounds while two of them (pܦ bܒ:) for some unknown reason were pronounced like the letter (ܘ) waw=w(ܦ: ܒ).

Of the six modified letters, five were modified simply by adding a dot underneath the letter, and one (ܦ) by merely adding a semi-circle attached below the letter (ܦ).

	Letters		Pronounced As		Example	
1-	ܒ	b	ܒ	wa		Hope	ܣܒܪܐ
2-	ܓ	g	ܓ	gha		Body	ܦܓܪܐ
3-	ܕ	d̲	ܕ	d̲a	in mother	Altar	ܡܕܒܚܐ
4-	ܟ	k	ܟ	kha		Humble	ܡܟܝܟܐ
5-	ܦ	p	ܦ	w		Lentils	ܛܠܘܦܐ
6-	ܬ	t	ܬ	tha	in third	Virgin	ܒܬܘܠܬܐ

Note: Some writers use for the sound kh the letter ܚ **H** with thick dot above ܚ̇

example ܡܫܚܐ (Mishkha) oil

These six sounds are gathered in one word (BGHaD̲KPaTH)

(ܒ ܓ ܕ ܟ ܦ ܬ) ܒܓܕܟܦܬ

In Classical Aramaic, there are four sounds that have no precise English letters: GH ܓ / D̲ ܕ / KH ܟ / TH ܬ

13th: The five sounds used only in the Modern Aramaic

Similar to the six sounds that were added to the classical language, five additional sounds are added to the modern Aramaic-Chaldean alphabet. These five new sounds were also added because of the influence of foreign languages and were formed by modifying certain letters. (ܦ ܟ ܕ ܓ ܦ) These five sounds are gathered in one word (FaCHDHaJaV)

The following chart indicates these five new sounds in script and sound:

	Letters Sounds		Pronounced as	Examples	
1-	ܦ	f	ܦ̈	fa	Pepper	ܦܠܦܠܐ
2-	ܟ	ch	ܟ̰	cha	Bed	ܟ̰ܕܦܢܐ
3-	ܓ	dh	ܓ̰	dha	Park	ܦܪܕ̈ܝܣܐ
4-	ܓ	j	ܓ̰	ja	Grinding mill	ܓ̰ܪܝܐ
5-	ܦ	v	ܦ̮	va	Video	ܦ̮ܝܕܝܘ

8

- When any of these vowels ܙܩܵܦܵܐ : ܦܬܵܚܵܐ : ܙܠܵܡܵܐ ܩܲܫܝܵܐ : ܙܠܵܡܵܐ ܦܫܝܼܩܵܐ enter to one of these sounds ܒ : ܓ : ܕ : ܟ : ܬ : ܦ the dot of the sound is replaced by one dot in the following sounds ܒ : ܓ : ܕ : ܟ : ܬ : ܦ (In the sound F the dots are put **over the thick dot (ܦ̇)**

Sounds	ܒ	ܓ	ܕ	ܟ	ܬ	ܦ	ܦ
Vowels	ܙܩܵܦܵܐ	ܙܠܵܡܵܐ ܩܲܫܝܵܐ	ܦܬܵܚܵܐ	ܙܠܵܡܵܐ ܦܫܝܼܩܵܐ	ܙܠܵܡܵܐ ܦܫܝܼܩܵܐ	ܦܬܵܚܵܐ	ܙܠܵܡܵܐ ܦܫܝܼܩܵܐ
	ܛܵܒܹ̈ܐ	ܬܵܓܹ̈ܐ	ܬܲܠܡܝܼܕܹ̈ܐ	ܡܲܠܲܐܟܹ̈ܐ	ܝܵܬ݂ܹܒ	ܦܲܪܲܓ݂	ܦܵܬܝܼܢ
	Tawe	Taghe	Talmeede	Malakhe	Yathew	Faraj	Fatin
	good	crowns	students	angels	sitting	Proper name	Proper name

- In this book the Aramaic-Chaldean Transliteration symbols will be in parenthesis in the right side of the English word.
  Example: ܫܠܵܡܵܐ (Shlama) Peace.

- When one word in English has more than one meaning in Chaldean, this sign (/) separates the English transliteration. And in Aramaic this sign (:) is generally used to indicate a comma and sometimes a semi-colon. (.) is generally used to indicate a full stop.
- Some grammarians add a dot over the following letters b ܒ̇ / g ܓ̇ /d ܕ̇ / k ܟ̇/ t ܬ̇ to indicate that the letter is pronounced hard (not soft)

14th: The addition of the letter A

Unpronounced letter A (ܐ) is added after any final letter in the word with one of the following three vowels:

	Vowels		Examples		
1-	Sqapa	ܙܩܵܦܵܐ	ܡܲܠܟܵܐ	Malka	King
2-	Zlama psheeqa	ܙܠܵܡܵܐ ܦܫܝܼܩܵܐ	ܢܸܗܘܹܐ	Tehwe	let it be
3-	Zlama qashya (Long E)	ܙܠܵܡܵܐ ܩܲܫܝܵܐ	ܡܲܠܟܹ̈ܐ	Malkay	Kings

15th: Two ways of writing letters ܓ G and ܬ T

The Aramaic writer may choose to write the letter G and the letter T in either of the following shapes:

Letter	First shape	Second shape
G	Gamal (ܓ)	ܓ
T	Taw (ܬ)	ܬ

16th: Eight Aramaic letters each takes a dot in writing

The thick dot is added on the top of the stroke of eight letters in writing, but only on the top and bottom of the stroke of the letter G only. When writing the alphabet by hand, there are eight letters that receive a large dot on the stroke, and in the case of the letter G (ܓ) the large dot is put on the top and the bottom of the stroke.

	1	2	3	4	5	6	7	8
Typewriter	ܐ	ܓ	ܚ	ܛ	ܢ	ܥ	ܨ	ܫ
Hand writing	ܐ	ܓ	ܚ	ܛ	ܢ	ܥ	ܨ	ܫ

17th: The Estrangela Letters ܐܣܛܪܢܓܠܐ

Out of the 22 alphabet letters, the following six letters have a different shape when writing in Estrangela:

ܠ ܗ̇ ܥ ܛ ܚ ، ܗ (ܗ) (ܪ) ܠ ܒ (ܐ)

(ܬ) ܫ (ܪ) ܡ ، ܩ ܠ ܩ ܡ (ܢ)

	Letters			Examples		
1.	A	ܐ	ܐ	ܐ	ܐܒ	Ab	August
2.	D	ܕ	ܪ	ܪ	ܕܪܐ	Dara	Century
3.	H	ܗ	ܗ	ܗ	ܐܠܗܐ	Alaha	God
4.	M	ܡ	ܡ	ܡ	ܡܪܝܡ	Mariam	Mary
5.	R	ܪ	ܪ	ܪ	ܪܒܐ	Raba	Great
6.	T	ܬ	ܬ	ܬ	ܬܪܒܝܬܐ	Tarbeetha	Education

18th: Doubling ܬܪܥܨܦܐ ܕܩ̈ܠܐ

These three vowels: **Short A** (ܲ), **Short I** (ܸ), **Long U** (ܘ) are considered short vowels and usually when a letter with a vowel follows them, in some words each one of them doubles in sound and never in

10

writing. After short A (÷) Example:ﻃﺒﺦ:(Tabaha) chef. After short I
(̤)Example: ﻟﺒﺎ (Lebba) heart/ After U (ﻭ) Ex ﺣﺒﺎ (Hubba) Love.

19th: The Suppressor ܡܫܬܩܢܐ

When a slanted line is placed above certain letters, it indicates that
the letter is silent. Example: (ﻥ) ܢܫܐ (Nasha) human also (ﺕ) example:
ܐܢܬ (at) you in Classical Aramaic.

20th: The Occulted Letters ܐܬܘܬܐ ܕܡܬܚܦܝܢ ܘܠܐ ܡܬܟܬܒܢ

There are three letters in Aramaic, Y (ܝ) W (ܘ) and D (ܕ) which
become silent but do not carry the suppressor sign.

Letters		Silent when used in	Examples		
Y	ܝ	a- singular possessive	ܡܠܟܟ	Malkakh	your king
		b- second person feminine	ܐܢܬܝ	A-yat	you
W	ܘ	verbs third person plural in past tense	ܐܙܠܘ	Iz–zal	they left
D	ܕ	word	ܥܕܬܐ	Ayta	church

21st: There are letters that are pronounced but not written: ܐܬܘܬܐ ܬܡܬܒܝܢ ܠܐ ܡܬܟܬܒܢ ܘܬܕܝܥܝܢ ܡܬܟܬܒܢ

The vowels (ܿ) and (ܘ) are pronounced but not written in the word ܟܠ
all (kol or Kul)

a- When the word all ܟܠ (Kul) is alone or is added to the beginning of
   another word, the vowel (ܘ) is pronounced, ܟܠ (Kul) All, and to
   another: ܟܠܡܕܡ (Kulmiddem) Everything.

b- When the word All ܟܠ is added at the end of another word, the
   vowel (ܿ) is pronounced kol but not written. Example: ܡܪܐܟܠ (Ma-
   raykol) the Lord of all.

c- The word ܡܛܠ (Meṭol) because, in pronounciation the vowel(ܿ) is
   added.

11

22ⁿᵈ: The Aramaic - Chaldean Numbers ܡܸܢܝܵܢܹ̈ܐ

The Aramaic numbers from one (1) to four hundred (400) correspond to the 22 letters of the Aramaic alphabet.

The letters (ܐ) through (ܛ) are the single numbers 1-9. Beginning with (ܝ) (10) each succeeding letter is counted by tens until (ܨ) (90).

Beginning with (ܩ) (100) each succeeding letter is counted by hundreds until (ܬ) (400), the last number to be counted in this method is 499 (ܬܨܛ) when writing compound numbers the large number should be first.

Example:	11=ܝܐ	22=ܟܒ	500=ܬܩ	501=ܬܩܐ	600=ܬܪ
	700=ܬܫ	800=ܬܬ	900=ܬܬܩ	999=ܬܬܩܨܛ	

There are many methods for writing thousands, one of which is: when one of the alphabet is first, it is counted one thousand, it is written with three dots over it 1000 (ܐ̈) 2000 (ܒ̈) Year 2011(ܒ̈ܝܐ). Or some writers add a straight line over the letter (ܐ̄) 1000 (ܒ̄) 2000

The Aramaic Numbers from 1–999

9=ܛ	8=ܚ	7=ܙ	6=ܘ	5=ܗ	4=ܕ	3=ܓ	2=ܒ	1=ܐ
18=ܝܚ	17=ܝܙ	16=ܝܘ	15=ܝܗ	14=ܝܕ	13=ܝܓ	12=ܝܒ	11=ܝܐ	10=ܝ
41=ܡܐ	40=ܡ	39=ܠܛ	31=ܠܐ	30=ܠ	29=ܟܛ	21=ܟܐ	20=ܟ	19=ܝܛ
71=ܥܐ	70=ܥ	69=ܣܛ	61=ܣܐ	60=ܣ	59=ܢܛ	51=ܢܐ	50=ܢ	49=ܡܛ
101=ܩܐ	100=ܩ	99=ܨܛ	91=ܨܐ	90=ܨ	89=ܦܛ	81=ܦܐ	80=ܦ	79=ܥܛ
600=ܬܪ	500=ܬܩ	400=ܬ	399=ܫܨܛ	300=ܫ	299=ܪܨܛ	200=ܪ	199=ܩܨܛ	111=ܩܝܐ
	999=ܬܬܩܨܛ			900=ܬܬܩ		800=ܬܬ	700=ܬܫ	

12

23rd : Quiz #1

Name in Chaldean the following 22 alphabet, 11 sounds, 7 vowels, and 6 Estrangela letters:

1- ܝ	14- ܒ	27- ܬ	40- ܐ
2- ܠ	15- ܗ	28- ܒ	41- ܠ
3- ܝ	16- ܩ	29- ܦ	42- ܓ
4- ܕ	17- ܪ	30- ܓ	43- ܡ
5- ܩ	18- ܓ	31- ܗ	44- ܨ
6- ܡ	19- ܠ	32- ܒ	45- ܝ
7- ܚ	20- ܣ	33- ܚ	46- ܢ
8- ܘ	21- ܨ	34- ܘ	47- ܠ
9- ܟ	22- ܘ	35- ܟ	48- ܢ
10- ܠ	23- ܘ	36- ܦ	49- ܥ
11- ܬ	24- ܀	37- ܢ	50- ܢ
12- ܐ	25- ÷	38- ܚ	51- ܩ
13- ܠ	26- ܁	39- ܩ	

24ᵗʰ : Quiz #2

Read the following 22 letters, 11 sounds, 7 vowels, 3 final letters, 6 estrangela letters, 8 enjoining letters, 14 joining letters, 2 letters with different shapes, 8 letters with thick dots and Aramaic letters that are numbers with no zero.

22 Alphabet	11 Sounds	7 Vowels	3 Letters have different finals	6 Estrangela Letters	8 Enjoining letters	14 Joining letters	2 Letters with different shapes	8 Letters take thick dot on the top.	Aramaic letters are Numbers with no Zero
1- ܐ		݈		ܐ	ܐ			ܐ	1 ܐ
2- ܒ	ܒ	݇				ܒ			2 ܒ
3- ܓ	ܓ ܓ	݉				ܓ	ܔ	ܓ	3 ܓ
4- ܕ	ܕ	݊		ܕ	ܕ				4 ܕ
5- ܗ		̇		ܗ	ܗ				5 ܗ
6- ܘ		̇			ܘ				6 ܘ
7- ܙ		̇			ܙ				7 ܙ
8- ܚ						ܚ		ܚ	8 ܚ
9- ܛ						ܛ		ܛ	9 ܛ
10- ܝ						ܝ		ܝ	10 ܝ
11- ܟ	ܟ ܟ	ܟ ܟ				ܟ			20 ܟ
12- ܠ						ܠ		ܠ	30 ܠ
13- ܡܟ		ܡ	ܡ			ܡ			40 ܡ
14- ܢ		ܢ ܢ				ܢ		ܢ	50 ܢ
15- ܣ						ܣ			60 ܣ
16- ܥ						ܥ		ܥ	70 ܥ
17- ܦ	ܦܦ					ܦ			80 ܦ
18- ܨ	ܨ				ܨ				90 ܨ
19- ܩ						ܩ			100 ܩ
20- ܪ				ܪ	ܪ				200 ܪ
21- ܫ						ܫ			300 ܫ
22- ܬ	ܬ			ܬ	ܬ		ܬ		400 ܬ

14

Chapter Two ܦܪܩܐ ܒ

Pronouns and Verbs ܚܠܦ ܫܡܗ̈ܐ ܘܡܠ̈ܐ

Modern Aramaic-Chaldean dialect has a masculine and a feminine form of "you," which means the sentence will change slightly depending on when you are talking masculine singular or feminine singular. In Modern Aramaic there is no word for dual form. Instead, the word "two" precedes the plural form, example: ܬܪܐ ܡܠܟ̈ܐ (Treh Malkeh) two kings.

Note: Please notice, "m" stands for masculine, small "f" stands for feminine, small "s" stands for singular, small "p" stands for plural.

1st: Pronouns ܚܠܦ ܫܡܗ̈ܐ

1- Personal Pronouns

1st Person	m/f:	I	ܐܢܐ	ana	pl:	we	ܐܚܢܢ	akhni
2nd Person	male:	you	ܐܢܬ	ayit	female:	you	ܐܢܬܝ	ayat
					pl, m/f:	you	ܐܢܬܘ(ܢ)	akhtu (N)
3rd Person	male:	he	ܐܗܘܘ	a-wu	female:	she	ܐܗܝ	a-yi
					pl, m/f:	they	ܐܢܗܝ	any

2- Possessive Suffix Pronouns

The possessive case is indicated in eight ways by adding one of the following suffixletters to a noun:

1-	long e	ܝ	2-	n	ܢ	3-	ukh	ܐܘܟ	4-	akh	ܐܟܝ
5-	okhun	ܐܘܟܘܢ	6-	ye	ܝܗ	7-	ah	ܐܗ	8-	yayi	ܗܝ

Example: garden ܒܣܬܢܐ (bistana). My garden bistani ܒܣܬܢܝ bistani

1st Person	m/f:	my (garden)	iong e	ܝ	ܒܣܬܢܝ	bistani
	Pl, m/f:	our (garden)	n	ܢ	ܒܣܬܢܢ	bistanan
2nd Person	m:	your (garden)	ukh	ܘܟ	ܒܣܬܢܘܟ	bistanukh
	f:	your (garden)	akh	ܟܝ	ܒܣܬܢܟܝ	bistanakh
	pl m&f	your (garden)	okhu (n)	(ܘܟܘ)(ܢ)	ܒܣܬܢܘܟܘ(ܢ)	bistanokhun

3rd person		m:	his (garden)	eh	ܗ	ܒܝܣܬܢܗ	bistaneh
		f:	her (garden)	ah	ܗ̇	ܒܝܣܬܢܗ̇	bistanah
		pl, m&f	their (garden)	yi	ܢܝ	ܒܝܣܬܢܢܝ	bistanayi

2nd: Verbs ܡܠܐ

The majority of Modern Aramaic verbs are derived from root words that generally consist of either two letters, for example: to fast: ܨܝܡ = ܨܝܢܐ (ṣam) or three letters for example: to work: ܦܠܝܚܐ = ܦܠܚ (plaḥ) or four letters, for example: to translate: ܬܪܓܡ = ܡܬܪܓܡܢܐ (targem).

There are four main tenses: 1- Past tense ܙܒܢܐ ܕܥܒܪ **2- Present tense** ܙܒܢܐ ܕܩܐܡ **3- Future tense** ܙܒܢܐ ܕܥܬܝܕ **4- The conjunctive /imperative/ order.** ܦܘܩܕܢܐ **. These tenses differ according to gender, number, and person.**

Note: The plural of the word verb ܡܠܬܐ (miltha) is ܡܠܐ (mille).

A - The verb to be (eeleh) ܕܐܝܬܘܗܝ

1- Past Tense

1st Person:	ms:	I was	ana winwa	ܐܢܐ ܘܝܢܘܐ
	fs:	I was	ana wanwa	ܐܢܐ ܘܢܘܐ
	m&f plural:	we were	akhny wukhwa	ܐܚܢܢ ܘܟܘܐ
2nd Person:	ms:	you were	ayit wutwa	ܐܝܬ ܘܬܘܐ
	fs:	you were	ayat watwa	ܐܝܬ ܘܬܘܐ
	m&f plural:	you were	akhtu wotuwa	ܐܚܬܘ ܘܬܘܐ
3rd Person:	ms:	he was	awu waywa	ܐܘ ܘܝܘܐ
	fs:	she was	ayi wawa	ܐܝ ܘܘܐ
	m&f plural:	they were	any wawa	ܐܢܝ ܘܘܐ

2- Present Tense

1st Person:	ms:	I am	ana eewin	ܐܢܐ ܐܝܘܝܢ
	fs:	I am	ana eewan	ܐܢܐ ܐܝܘܢ
	m&f plural:	we are	akhny eewukh	ܐܚܢܢ ܐܝܘܟ

2nd Person:	ms:	you are	ayit eewit	ܐ̄ܝܬ ܐܝܘܝܬ
	fs:	you are	ayat eewat	ܐ̄ܝܬ ܐܝܘܘܬ
3rd Person:	m&f plural:	you are	akhtu wotu	ܐܚܬܘ ܘܬܘ
	ms:	he is	awu eeleh	ܐܘܘ ܐܝܠܗ
	fs:	she is	ayi eelah	ܐܝܝ ܐܝܠܗ
	m&f plural:	they are	any eelay	ܐܢܝ ܐܝܠܝ

3- Future Tense

1st Person:	ms:	I will be	ana bidhawin	ܐܢܐ ܒܕܗܘܝܢ
	fs:	I will be	ana bidhoyan	ܐܢܐ ܒܕܗܘܝܢ
	m&f plural:	we will be	akhny bidhawukh	ܐܚܢܝ ܒܕܗܘܘܟ
2nd Person:	ms:	you will be	ayit bidhawit	ܐ̄ܝܬ ܒܕܗܘܝܬ
	fs:	you will be	ayat bidhoyat	ܐ̄ܝܬ ܒܕܗܘܝܬ
	m&f plural:	you will be	akhtu bidhawotu	ܐܚܬܘ ܒܕܗܘܘܬܘ
3rd Person:	ms:	he will be	awu bidhawe	ܐܘܘ ܒܕܗܘܐ
	fs:	she will be	ayi bidhoyah	ܐܝܝ ܒܕܗܘܝܗ
	m&f plural:	they will be	anyi bidhaway	ܐܢܝ ܒܕܗܘܝ

4- Order Tense/ Imperative

1st Person:	ms:	I should be	ana shud hawin	ܐܢܐ ܫܘܕ ܗܘܝܢ
	or		ana shud payshin	ܐܢܐ ܫܘܕ ܦܝܫܝܢ
	fs:	I should be	ana shud hoyan	ܐܢܐ ܫܘܕ ܗܘܝܢ
	m&f plural:	we should be	akhny shud hawukh	ܐܚܢܝ ܫܘܕ ܗܘܘܟ
2nd Person:	ms:	you should be	ayit shud hawit	ܐ̄ܝܬ ܫܘܕ ܗܘܝܬ
	or		ayit hwi	ܐ̄ܝܬ ܗܘܝ
	fs:	you should be	ayat shud hoyat	ܐ̄ܝܬ ܫܘܕ ܗܘܝܬ
	or		ayat hweh	ܐ̄ܝܬ ܗܘܗ
	m&f plural:	you should be	akhtu shud hawotu	ܐܚܬܘ ܫܘܕ ܗܘܘܬܘ
	or		akhtu hwo	ܐܚܬܘ ܗܘܘ
3rd Person:	ms:	he should be	awu shud hawe	ܐܘܘ ܫܘܕ ܗܘܐ
	fs:	she should be	ayi shud hoyah	ܐܝܝ ܫܘܕ ܗܘܝܗ
	m&f plural:	they should be	any shud haway	ܐܢܝ ܫܘܕ ܗܘܝ

17

B- The verb to wait ܣܦ̈ܝܪܗ (spayreh)

1-The Past Tense

1st Person:	(ms):	I waited	(ana spayry)	ܐܢܐ ܣܦܝܪܝ
	(fs):	I waited	(ana spayry)	ܐܢܐ ܣܦܝܪܝ
	m&f plural:	we waited	(akhny spayran)	ܐܚܢܢ ܣܦ̈ܝܪܢ
2nd Person:	(ms):	you waited	(ayit spayrukh)	ܐܝܬ ܣܦ̈ܝܪܘܟ
	(fs):	you waited	(ayat spayrakh)	ܐܝܬܝ ܣܦ̈ܝܪܟܝ
	m&f plural:	you waited	(akhtu spayrokhu)	ܐܚܬܘ ܣܦ̈ܝܪܟܘ
3rd Person:	(ms):	he waited	(awu spayreh)	ܐܘܘ ܣܦ̈ܝܪܗ
	(fs):	she waited	(ayi spayrah)	ܐܝܝ ܣܦ̈ܝܪܗ
	m&f plural:	they waited	(any spayray)	ܐܢܝ ܣܦ̈ܝܪܝ

2-The Present Tense

1st Person:	(ms):	I am waiting	ana eewin bespara	ܐܢܐ ܐܝܘܢ ܒܣܦܪܐ
	(fs):	I am waiting	ana eewan bespara	ܐܢܐ ܐܝܘܢ ܒܣܦܪܐ
	m&f plural:	we are waiting	akhny eewukh bespara	ܐܚܢܢ ܐܝܘܟ ܒܣܦܪܐ
2nd Person:	(ms):	you are waiting	ayit eewit bespara	ܐܝܬ ܐܝܘܬ ܒܣܦܪܐ
	(fs):	you are waiting	ayat eewat bespara	ܐܝܬܝ ܐܝܘܬܝ ܒܣܦܪܐ
	m&f plural:	you are waiting	akhtu wotu bespara	ܐܚܬܘ ܘܬܘ ܒܣܦܪܐ
3rd Person:	(ms):	he is waiting	awu eeleh bespara	ܐܘܘ ܐܝܠܗ ܒܣܦܪܐ
	(fs):	she is waiting	ayi eelah bespara	ܐܝܝ ܐܝܠܗ ܒܣܦܪܐ
	m&f plural:	they are waiting	any eelay bespara	ܐܢܝ ܐܝܠܝ ܒܣܦܪܐ

3-The Future Tense

1st Person:	(ms):	I will wait	ana bsaprin	ܐܢܐ ܒܣܦܪܝܢ
	or	I will wait	ana zeelin bsbapran	ܐܢܐ ܘܝܠܝ ܒܣܦܪܢ
	(fs):	I will wait	ana bsbapran	ܐܢܐ ܒܣܦܪܢ
	m&f plural:	we will wait	akhny bsaprukh	ܐܚܢܢ ܒܣܦܪܘܟ
2nd Person:	(ms):	you will wait	ayit bsaprit	ܐܝܬ ܒܣܦܪܬ
	(fs):	you will wait	ayat bsaprat	ܐܝܬܝ ܒܣܦܪܬܝ
	m&f plural:	you will wait	akhtu bsaprootu	ܐܚܬܘ ܒܣܦܪܘܬܘ
3rd Person:	(ms):	he will wait	ahoo bsapir	ܐܘܘ ܒܣܦܪ
	(fs):	she will wait	ayi bsaprah	ܐܝܝ ܒܣܦܪܗ
	m&f plural:	they will wait	anyi bsapry	ܐܢܝ ܒܣܦܪܝ

4-The Conjunctive Imperative (Order) Tense

1st Person:	(ms):	I should wait	ana shud saprin	ܐܢܐ ܫܘܕ ܣܦܪܝܢ
	(fs):	I should wait	ana shud sapran	ܐܢܐ ܫܘܕ ܣܦܪܢ
m&f plural:		we should wait	akhny shud saprukh	ܐܚܢܝ ܫܘܕ ܣܦܪܘܟ
2nd Person:	(ms):	you should wait	ayit shud saprit	ܐܝܬ ܫܘܕ ܣܦܪܝܬ
or (ms):		wait	spor	ܣܦܘܪ
	(fs):	you should wait	ayat shud saprat	ܐܝܬܝ ܫܘܕ ܣܦܪܬܝ
or (fs):		wait	spor	ܣܦܘܪܝ
m&f plural:		we should wait	akhtu shud saprutu	ܐܚܬܘ ܫܘܕ ܣܦܪܘܬܘ
	or	wait	sporo	ܣܦܘܪܘ
3rd Person:	(ms):	he should wait	awoh shud sapir	ܐܘܗ ܫܘܕ ܣܦܪ
	(fs):	she should wait	ayi shud saprah	ܐܝܗ ܫܘܕ ܣܦܪܗ
m&f plural:		they should wait	anyi shud sapry	ܐܢܝܗ ܫܘܕ ܣܦܪܝ

Chaldean Hunter

Chapter Three ܡܸܢܕܝܵܐ ܓ

Chaldean Dialogue ܗܘܵܠܵܐ ܘܫܸܩܠܵܐ
(H-wala W-shqala)
Read, write, and speak modern Aramaic-Chaldean dialect
ܩܪܝ : ܟܬܼܘܒ : ܘܡܲܗܟܹܐ ܠܸܫܵܢܵܐ ܐܵܪܵܡܵܝܵܐ ܚܲܕܬܼܵܐ ܒܠܝܼܐܵܙܵܐ ܟܲܠܕܵܝܵܐ
(Qree, kthu, w-mahke, lushana Aramaya khatha bli-aza kaldaya)

Notes:

- The modern Aramaic-Chaldean dialect of the cities in the plains of the Nineveh region in the north of Mesopotamia-Iraq is being used.

- When one word has more than one meaning in Chaldean, this sign (/) separates the English transliteration. And in Aramaic, this sign (:) separates many meanings.

Useful phrases ܡܲܚܟ̈ܘܝܹ ܥܡܝܕ ܟܸܢ̈ܢܹ

(Maḥkoye Immid khenne)

1st: Meetings ܟܢܝܫܘܼܬܵ : ܚܙܵܝܵ ܕܢܵܫܹ : ܗ ܦܩܵ ܕܢܵܫܹ

(kneeshootha/khzaya d-nashe/tfaqa b-nashe)

1. Greeting (Draya dishlama) ܕܪܵܐ ܕܸܫܠܵܡܵ
2. Hello/Hi (Shlama) ܫܠܵܡܵ
3. Welcome (Bshayna) ܒܫܲܝܢܵ
4. Goodbye (Posh bashlama) or (See alaha emmukh)
   ܦܘܿܫ ܒܫܠܵܡܵ : ܗܒ ܐܲܠܵܗܵ ܥܡܘܿܟ

2nd: The use of the word "peace" in Aramaic-Chaldean

The word (Shlama) peace ܫܠܵܡܵ is used to greet both in daytime as well as at nighttime.

Note: The English word means "onto you" is in Aramaic-Chaldean uses illid (ܥܸܠܸܕ) but when it is used with possessive pronoun it loses the final letter D.

To say "onto you" becomes ܥܸܠܸܗܝ as is in the example shown below: <u>the singular masculine</u> possessive pronoun one vowel and sound (ukh ܘܟ) are added when the second person is male "peace be on to you" (shlama ellukh) ܫܠܵܡܵ ܥܸܠܘܿܟ

<u>With the singular feminine</u> possessive pronoun one sound and one letter (akh ܟܝ) are added when the second person is female "onto you" (Shlama ellakh) ܫܠܵܡܵ ܥܸܠܵܟܝ

<u>With plural masculine and feminine</u> possessive pronoun one sound, one vowel, and one letter (khun ܟܘܢ) are added "to you" (shlama ellokhun) ܫܠܵܡܵ ܥܸܠܵܟܘܼܢ

3rd: Essentials/ Gender   ܐܘܿܣܵܝܵܬ݂ܵܐ : ܓܸܢܣܹܐ

(Oseyatha/ Ginse)

1. How are you? (Dikh eewit/ ma minnukh?)

   ܕܝܼܟ݂ ܐܝܼܘܸܬ : ܡܵܐ ܡܸܢܘܿܟ݂

2. Fine (Tawa/ randa) ܛܵܒ݂ܵܐ : ܪܲܢܕܵܐ

3. And how about you? (MS: W-ayit?) ܘܐܲܝܸܬ (FM: W-ayat?) ܘܐܲܝܲܬ

4. My name is Daniel (Ana shemye eele Daniel) ܐܵܢܵܐ ܫܹܡܝܼ ܐܝܼܠܹܗ ܕܵܢܝܼܐܸܠ

5. What is your name? (meele shemukh?) ܡܹܠܹܗ ܫܹܡܘܿܟ݂

6. I am pleased to know you (Ana pseekha win d-kimyad-innukh)

   ܐܵܢܵܐ ܦܨܝܼܚܵܐ ܘܝܼܢ ܕܟܸܡܝܵܕܸܢܘܿܟ݂

7. Yes (Eh/ balayh/ should hawe/ hadakh eeleh)

   ܐܹ : ܒܲܠܹܐ : ܫܘܿܕ ܗܵܘܹܐ : ܗܵܕܲܟ݂ ܐܝܼܠܹܗ

8. No (La) ܠܵܐ

9. Maybe (Balky/ balkid) ܒܲܠܟܝܼ : ܒܲܠܟܝܼܕ

10. Please (In basmalukh/ kimnonin minnukh/ bkhairukh/ in ba-it/ khlapukh) ܐܸܢ ܒܵܣܡܵܠܘܿܟ݂ : ܟܹܡܢܘܿܢܸܢ ܡܸܢܘܿܟ݂ : ܒܟ݂ܲܝܪܘܿܟ݂ : ܐܸܢ ܒܵܥܹܝܬ : ܟ݂ܠܵܦܘܿܟ݂

11. Thank you (Basma gyanukh/ gyanukh basimta/ ktanin minta minnukh/ qurbanukh/ tawdy)

    ܒܵܣܡܵܐ ܓܝܵܢܘܿܟ݂ : ܓܝܵܢܘܿܟ݂ ܒܵܣܸܡܬܵܐ : ܟܬܵܢܸܢ ܡܸܢܬܵܐ ܡܸܢܘܿܟ݂ : ܩܘܿܪܒܵܢܘܿܟ݂ : ܬܵܘܕܝܼ

12. You are welcome (Bshaina bgawukh/ Bshaina thailukh)

    ܒܫܲܝܢܵܐ ܒܓܵܘܘܿܟ݂ : ܒܫܲܝܢܵܐ ܬܲܝܠܘܿܟ݂

13. You are very welcome (Bshayna w-beshlama/ bshayna wbtawatha)

    ܒܫܲܝܢܵܐ ܘܒܸܫܠܵܡܵܐ : ܒܫܲܝܢܵܐ ܘܒܬ݂ܵܘܵܬ݂ܵܐ

14. Excuse me (Shwoq Tali/ halli mafar/ La arit elli/ La payish libokh minni/ la jagrit minni)

    ܫܒ݂ܘܿܩ ܛܵܠܝܼ : ܗܲܠܠܝܼ ܡܵܦܲܪ : ܠܵܐ ܐܵܪܹܝܬ ܐܸܠܠܝܼ : ܠܵܐ ܦܵܝܸܫ ܠܸܒܘܿܟ݂ ܡܸܢܝܼ : ܠܵܐ ܔܵܓܪܝܼܬ ܡܸܢܝܼ

15. This is my friend (Ady eele khori) ܐܵܕܝܼ ܐܝܼܠܹܗ ܟ݂ܘܿܪܝܼ

16. This is my home telephone number (Adeele minyana dtelephone diyi dbaytha) ܐܵܕܝܼܠܹܗ ܡܸܢܝܵܢܵܐ ܕܛܹܠܹܦ݂ܘܿܢ ܕܝܼܝܼ ܕܒܲܝܬ݂ܵܐ

17. Mobile telephone (Telephone d-eeda) ܛܹܠܹܦ݂ܘܿܢ ܕܐܝܼܕܵܐ

18. This is my mobile number (Adeele minyana dtelephone diyi d-eeda) ܐܵܕܝܼܠܹܗ ܡܸܢܝܵܢܵܐ ܕܛܹܠܹܦ݂ܘܿܢ ܕܝܼܝܼ ܕܐܝܼܕܵܐ

19. Write it to me (Kthule ṭaly) ܟܬܘܒܝܠܗ ܛܠܝ
20. Much (Kabbeera) ܟܒܝܪܐ
21. Encountering (Malqoye/tfaqa) ܡܠܩܘܝܐ : ܗܦܩܐ

4ᵗʰ: Daily activities (Shoola d-kudyom) ܫܘܠܐ ܕܟܘܕܝܘܡ

1. Relax (Nyakha) ܢܝܚܐ
2. Daily newspaper (Spar yawma/Jareeda dyawma)
   ܣܦܪ ܝܘܡܐ : ܔܪܝܕܐ ܕܝܘܡܐ
3. Newspaper (Gazaitha/Jareeda/spar zawna)
   ܓܙܝܬܐ : ܔܪܝܕܐ : ܣܦܪ ܙܘܢܐ
4. Returning home (Eethaya/daara lbaytha) ܐܝܬܝܐ : ܕܐܪܐ ܠܒܝܬܐ
5. Going to bed (Awara le-shweetha) ܐܘܪܐ ܠܫܘܝܬܐ
6. Going to sleep (Dmakha) ܕܡܟܐ
7. Waking up (R-asha/qyama mshintha) ܪܥܫܐ : ܩܝܡܐ ܡܫܝܢܬܐ
8. Getting up (Qyama/ḥmala) ܩܝܡܐ : ܚܡܠܐ
9. Getting dressed (Lwasha djulle) ܠܘܫܐ ܔܘܠܬ
10. Taking the children to school (Nobole d-yale zore lescola/ lmadrashta) ܢܒܠܐ ܕܝܢܩܐ ܘܟܦܘܕܐ ܠܥܣܩܠܐ : ܠܡܕܪܫܬܐ
11. Picking up the children (Shqala/mothoye d-yale zore)
    ܫܩܠܐ : ܡܘܬܘܝܐ ܕܝܢܩܐ ܘܟܦܘܕܐ
12. Taking the bus to the market (Rcawa b-bus ta eezala lshuqa)
    ܪܟܒܐ ܒܒܘܣ ܬܐ ܐܙܠܐ ܠܫܘܩܐ
13. Driving to work (Eezala beṭrumbayl lshula/ Eezala B-markabtha lshula) ܐܙܠܐ ܒܛܪܘܡܒܝܠ ܠܫܘܠܐ : ܐܙܠܐ ܒܡܪܟܒܬܐ ܠܫܘܠܐ
14. Leaving work (Shwaqa/ plaṭa mshula) ܫܘܩܐ : ܦܠܛܐ ܡܫܘܠܐ
15. Cleaning the house (Mandhofe dbaytha) ܡܢܕܗܦܐ ܕܒܝܬܐ
16. Cooking dinner (Mahdhore a-ashaya) ܡܗܕܘܪܐ ܕܒܥܫܝܐ
17. Watching TV (Khyara/ mfaroje ltelevizion/ Press ḥezwa)
    ܚܝܪܐ : ܡܦܪܘܔܐ ܠܬܠܩܘܝܣ : ܦܪܣ ܚܙܘܐ
18. Doing homework (A-wada dwaleetha/A-wada dwajib dbaytha)
    ܥܒܕܐ ܕܘܠܝܬܐ : ܥܒܕܐ ܕܘܔܝܒ ܕܒܝܬܐ

23

5th: Breaking the language barrier ܡܲܚܩܘܿܝܹܐ ܥܸܡܸܕ ܟ݂ܸܢܹܐ
(Mahkoye immid khenne)

1. Can you speak English? (Ayit eebukh dmahkit Engelizi/Ayit eebukh dimtanit Engelezi?)

    ܐܝܹܐ ܐܝܒܘܿܟ݂ ܕܡܲܚܟܸܬ ܐܝܢܓܠܝܼܙܝܼ : ܐܝܹܐ ܐܝܒܘܿܟ݂ ܕܡܸܬܲܢܝܹܐ ܐܝܢܓܠܝܼܙܝܼ

2. Yes, I can speak English (Eh ana eebi dmahkin Engelizi/ Eh ana eebi d-mtanin Engelizi

    ܐܹܐ ܐܵܢܵܐ ܐܝܒܼܝ ܕܡܲܚܟܸܢ ܐܝܢܓܠܝܼܙܝܼ : ܐܹܐ ܐܵܢܵܐ ܐܝܒܼܝ ܕܡܸܬܲܢܝܼ ܐܝܢܓܠܝܼܙܝܼ

3. Do you understand? (Ayit kdarkit/ Ayit kfahmit/ Ayit kyadit?)

    ܐܝܹܐ ܟܕܲܪܟܸܬ : ܐܝܹܐ ܟܦܲܗܡܸܬ : ܐܝܹܐ ܟܝܲܕܝܼܬ؟

4. No, I do not understand (La ana la kdarkin/ La ana la kfahmit/ La ana la lakyadin).

    ܠܵܐ ܐܵܢܵܐ ܠܵܐ ܟܕܲܪܟܸܢ :ܠܵܐ ܐܵܢܵܐ ܠܵܐ ܟܦܲܗܡܸܬ : ܠܵܐ ܐܵܢܵܐ ܠܵܐ ܟܝܲܕܝܼܡ

5. I speak a little Chaldean language (Ana kmahkin (Kha) qesa leshana kaldaya) ܐܵܢܵܐ ܟܡܲܚܟܸܢ(ܚܵܐ) ܩܸܣܵܐ ܠܸܫܵܢܵܐ ܟܲܠܕܵܝܵܐ

6. Where are you from? (Ayit min aika wit?) ܐܝܹܐ ܡܸܢ ܐܲܝܟܵܐ ܐܝܬ

7. I am from San Diego (Ana eewin min San Diego) ܐܵܢܵܐ ܐܝܘܝܼܢ ܡܸܢ ܣܵܢ ܕܝܼܐܓܘ

8. Personal details (Tanayatha parsopayatha/ preeshe)

    ܬܲܢܵܝܵܬ݂ܵܐ ܦܲܪܨܘܿܦܵܝܵܬ݂ܵܐ : ܦܪܝܼܫܹܐ

9. Where were you born? (Ayit aica wutwa huya? B-ayma duktha wutwa huya?) ܐܝܹܐ ܐܲܝܟܵܐ ܘܘܼܬܘܵܐ ܗܘܿܝܵܐ؟ ܒܐܲܝܡܵܐ ܕܘܿܟ݂ܬ݂ܵܐ ܘܘܼܬܘܵܐ ܗܘܿܝܵܐ؟

10. I was born in Mesopotamia (Ana wunwa hooya b-beth Nahreen)

    ܐܵܢܵܐ ܘܘܼܢܘܵܐ ܗܘܿܝܵܐ ܒܒܹܝܬ݂ ܢܲܗܪܹܝܢ

11. Slowly (Neekha/ haydy/ bhamdukh/ bish yaqura/ La labkit/ yawash/ lkayfukh)

    ܢܝܼܚܵܐ : ܗܲܝܕܝܼ : ܒܚܲܡܕܘܿܟ݂ : ܒܸܫ ܝܲܩܘܿܪܵܐ : ܠܵܐ ܠܲܒܟܸܬ : ܝܵܘܵܫ : ܠܟܲܝܦܘܿܟ݂

6th: The Family ܢܲܫܘܵܬ݂ܵܐ : ܐܘܿܓ݂ܵܓ݂
(Nashwatha/ojagh)

1. Father (Baba) ܒܵܒܵܐ

2. Mother (Yimma) ܝܸܡܵܐ

3. Brother (Akhona) ܐܲܚܘܿܢܵܐ

4. Sister (Khatha) ܚܵܬܼܵܐ

5. Child – boy (Ayala zora/ aajy/ Tifla) ܝܵܠܵܐ ܘܟܼܘܵܕܵܐ : ܢܓܼܝܼܕ : ܝܼܦܠܵܐ

6. Child – girl (Ayalta zorta/ Tefiltha) ܝܵܠܬܵܐ ܘܟܼܘܵܕܬܵܐ : ܝܼܦܠܬܼܵܐ

7. Young (Zora(m)/ zorta(f) ܘܟܼܘܵܕܵܐ : ܘܟܼܘܵܕܬܵܐ

8. Young girl (Khamtha/ brata) ܫܵܡܬܼܵܐ : ܒܼܪܵܬܵܐ

9. Young boy (Jwanqa/ A-laima) ܓܼܘܵܢܩܵܐ : ܥܠܲܝܡܵܐ

10. Husband/ Man (Gora) ܓܼܘܼܪܵܐ

11. Woman (Bakhta) ܒܲܟܼܬܵܐ

12. Wife (Bakhta) ܒܲܟܼܬܵܐ

13. Parents Dad & Mom (Baba w-yimma) ܒܵܒܵܐ ܘܝܼܡܵܐ

14. Todler/ Baby (Masculine) (tifla) ܝܼܦܠܵܐ / (Feminine) (tifiltha) ܝܼܦܠܬܼܵܐ

15. Son (Brona) ܒܼܪܘܿܢܵܐ

16. Boy (Brona/ Talia) ܒܼܪܘܿܢܵܐ : ܛܲܠܝܵܐ

17. Daughter (Brata) ܒܼܪܵܬܵܐ

18. Girl (Brata/ Tleetha) ܒܼܪܵܬܵܐ : ܛܠܝܼܬܼܵܐ

19. Nephew: Son of brother/ sister (Brona d-khatha/ ber d-akhona)
ܒܼܪܘܿܢܵܐ ܕܚܵܬܼܵܐ : ܒܲܪ ܕܐܲܚܘܿܢܵܐ

20. Niece: Daughter of sister (Brata d-khatha/ brata dakhona)
ܒܼܪܵܬܵܐ ܕܚܵܬܼܵܐ : ܒܼܪܵܬܵܐ ܕܐܲܚܘܿܢܵܐ

21. Grandmother (Saota/ dayi/ dada) ܣܵܘܬܼܵܐ : ܕܲܝܼ : ܕܵܕܵܐ

22. Grandfather (Sawa) ܣܵܒܼܵܐ

23. Senior citizen (Gora raba/ Bakhta rabtha b-aumra)
ܓܼܘܼܪܵܐ ܪܵܒܵܐ : ܒܲܟܼܬܵܐ ܪܲܒܬܼܵܐ ܒܥܘܼܡܪܵܐ

24. Old man (Gora sawa) ܓܼܘܼܪܵܐ ܣܵܒܼܵܐ

25. Old woman (Bakhta sota) ܒܲܟܼܬܵܐ ܣܵܒܼܬܼܵܐ

26. Uncle: brother of the mother (Khala) ܚܵܠܵܐ
    Uncle: brother of the father (Aamma) ܥܲܡܵܐ

27. Aunt: sister of the mother (Khalta) ܚܵܠܬܼܵܐ
    Aunt: sister of the father (Aamta) ܥܲܡܬܼܵܐ

28. Cousin: daughter of the mother's brother (Brata dkhala) ܒܪܵܬܐ ܕܚܵܠܐ

29. Bride (Kalu/ Kaltha) ܟܲܠܘ : ܟܲܠܬ݂ܐ

30. Groom (Khithna) ܚܸܬ݂ܢܐ

31. Son-in-law (Khithna) ܚܸܬ݂ܢܐ

32. Daughter-in-law (Kaltha) ܟܲܠܬ݂ܐ

33. Father-in-law (Khimyana) ܚܸܡܝܵܢܐ

34. Mother-in-law (khmatha) ܚܡܵܬ݂ܐ

35. Sister-in-law (Brakhmatha/ brakhma-a) ܒܲܪܚܡܵܬ݂ܐ : ܒܲܪܚܡܵܐ

36. Brother-in-law of the woman (Idma) ܝܕܡܵܐ

37. Two men married two sisters; each man is called (Adeela) ܐܵܕܝܼܠܐ

38. Two women married two brothers; each woman is called (Eedamtha) ܝܕܵܡܬ݂ܐ

39. Age (Aumra) ܥܘܼܡܪܐ

40. Attractive (Shapir hzatha/mar dimma haluya/gurjaya/jindaya) ܫܲܦܝܼܪ ܚܙܵܬ݂ܐ : ܡܵܪ ܕܸܡܵܐ ܚܲܠܘܼܝܐ : ܓܘܼܪܔܵܝܐ : ܔܝܼܢܕܵܝܐ

41. Average (Palgaya) ܦܲܠܓܵܝܐ

42. Heavyset (Milya/qsheeta/shammeena/treesa) ܡܝܼܠܝܐ : ܩܫܝܼܬ݂ܐ : ܫܲܡܝܼܢܐ : ܬܪܝܼܣܐ

43. Handsome (Khelya/halooya/shapeera) ܚܸܠܝܐ : ܚܲܠܘܼܝܐ : ܫܲܦܝܼܪܐ

44. I am, your son I love you Dad (Ana eewin bronukh, ana kybinnukh Baba) ܐܵܢܐ ܐܝܼܘܸܢ ܒܪܘܿܢܘܼܟ݂ : ܐܵܢܐ ܟܹܒܸܢܘܼܟ݂ ܒܵܒܐ

45. I am your son, I love you Mom (Ana eewin bronakh, kybinnakh Yimma) ܐܵܢܐ ܐܝܼܘܸܢ ܒܪܘܿܢܵܟ݂ : ܟܹܒܸܢܵܟ݂ ܝܸܡܐ

46. I am your daughter, I love you Dad (Ana eewan bratukh kybannukh Baba) ܐܵܢܐ ܐܝܼܘܲܢ ܒܪܵܬܘܼܟ݂ : ܟܹܒܲܢܘܼܟ݂ ܒܵܒܐ

47. I am your daughter, I love you Mom (Ana eewan bratakh kybannakh Mom) ܐܵܢܐ ܐܝܼܘܲܢ ܒܪܵܬܵܟ݂ : ܟܹܒܲܢܵܟ݂ ܝܸܡܐ

48. I missed you (Dukthukh eela spiqta) ܕܘܼܟܬ݂ܘܼܟ݂ ܝܼܠܵܗ ܣܦܝܼܩܬ݂ܐ

49. Physically challenged/ Disabled (Saqat/ ateela/ Ad d-laibeh drakhish) ܣܲܩܲܛ : ܐܵܬܹܝܠܐ : ܐܵܕ ܕܠܲܝܒܹܗ ܕܪܵܟ݂ܸܫ

50. Pregnant (Btynta/ yaqurta) ܒܛܝܼܢܬ݂ܐ : ܝܲܩܘܼܪܬ݂ܐ

51. Short (Kerya/ Quṯa/ Shkutta) ܩܛܢܐ : ܩܘܛܐ : ܫܟܘܛܐ

52. Sight impaired (Simya/ kora) ܣܡܝܐ : ܟܘܪܐ

53. Blind (Aawara) ܥܘܪܐ

54. Thin/ slim (Qaṯeena/ Dha-aeef/ naheewa) ܢܚܝܒܐ : ܢܚܝܒ : ܢܚܝܘܐ

55. He loves (Awo Kybeh/ Awo k-hayib) ܐܵܗܘ ܟܝܒܗ : ܐܵܗܘ ܟܚܝܒ

56. She loves (kyba/ k-hayba) ܟܝܒܐ ܟܚܝܒܐ : ܟܝܒܐ ܟܚܝܒܐ

57. To Fall in love (Npala bhubba/ ashaqa) ܢܦܠܐ ܒܚܘܒܐ : ܥܫܩܐ

58. Hearing impaired/ deaf (Tarsha/ karra) ܛܪܫܐ : ܟܪܐ

7th: School ܡܕܪܫܬܐ : ܐܣܟܘܠܐ
(Madrashta/ eskola)

1. Office (Duktha d-plakha) ܕܘܟܬܐ ܕܦܠܟܐ

2. Cafeteria (Ductha d-eekhala) ܕܘܟܬܐ ܕܐܝܟܠܐ

3. Computer (computer) ܟܘܡܦܝܘܬܪ

4. Library (Beth Arke/ baitha d-kthawane)
   ܒܝܬ ܐܪܟܐ : ܒܝܬܐ ܕܟܬܒܢܐ

5. Multipurpose room (Qubba de-plakha) ܩܘܒܐ ܕܦܠܟܐ

6. Listening (Maṣothe/ shma-a) ܡܨܘܬܐ : ܫܡܥܐ

7. Notebook (Daftar/ penqeetha) ܕܦܬܪ : ܦܢܩܝܬܐ

8. Playground (Darta d-ṯa-aooleh) ܕܪܬܐ ܕܛܥܠܐ

9. Type (Ṯba-aa) ܛܒܥܐ

10. Writing (Bikthawa) ܒܟܬܒܐ

11. Coming (Eethaya) ܐܝܬܝܐ

12. Entering (Iwara) ܥܒܪܐ

13. Going (Eezala) ܐܙܠܐ

14. Closing (Ghlaqa) ܓܠܩܐ

15. Leaving (Sayobe d-duktha / Eezala) ܫܒܩ ܕܘܟܬܐ : ܐܙܠܐ

16. Drawing (Rsama) ܪܣܡܐ

17. Raising one hand (Ma-aloye d-eeda) ܡܥܠܘܝܐ ܕܐܝܕܐ

18. Reading (Qraya) ܩܪܝܐ

19. Tearing (Jyaqa) ܓܝܩܐ

8th: Classroom ܩܘܒܐ ܕܝܕܪܫܐ

(Qubba didrasa)

1. Student (Talmeeda/ scolaya/ yalopa)
   ܬܠܡܝܕܐ : ܣܟܘܠܝܐ : ܝܠܘܦܐ

2. Teacher (Malpana/rabi) ܡܠܦܢܐ : ܪܒܝ

3. Book (Kthawa) ܟܬܒܐ

4. Chapter (Qaypaleon) ܩܦܠܐܘܢ

5. Bookcase (Chanta dekthawane) ܟܢܬܐ ܕܟܬܒܢܐ

6. Bulletin board (Loha dim-aeeranutha) ܠܘܚܐ ܕܡܐܥܪܢܘܬܐ

7. Chalk (Tabasheer) ܛܒܫܝܪ

8. Chalkboard (Loha/ sabura) ܠܘܚܐ : ܣܒܘܪܐ

9. Clock (Shaytha) ܫܥܬܐ

10. Desk (Mais dikthawa) ܡܝܣ ܕܟܬܒܐ

11. Table (Mays) ܡܝܣ

12. Eraser (Mashaya) ܡܫܝܐ

13. Flag (Atha/ bayraq/ neesha/ aalam) ܐܬܐ : ܟܬܒ : ܢܝܫܐ : ܒܝܪܩ : ܥܠܡ

14. Glue (Dabuqana/ simigh) ܕܒܘܩܢܐ : ܣܡܝܓ

15. Lock (Qifil/ dora) ܩܦܠܐ : ܕܘܪܐ

16. Markers (Qalama dersama) ܩܠܡܐ ܕܪܫܡܐ

17. Paper/ Loose-leaf (Waraqa) ܘܪܩܐ

18. Pen (qalama dhubir) ܩܠܡܐ ܕܚܒܪ

19. Pencil (Qalama dreses) ܩܠܡܐ ܕܪܫܝܫ

20. Ruler (Mastara/knonta) ܡܣܛܪܐ : ܟܢܘܢܬܐ

21. Sharpener (Mshapyana) ܡܫܦܝܢܐ

22. Give a speech (Hwala dmahkaytha/ makroze)
    ܗܘܠܐ ܕܡܚܟܝܬܐ : ܡܟܪܘܙܐ

The Lord's Prayer in Estrangela Script in Classical Aramaic

ܐܒܘܢ ܕܒܫܡܝܐ܁ ܢܬܩܕܫ ܫܡܟ܁ ܬܐܬܐ ܡܠܟܘܬܟ܁ ܢܗܘܐ
ܨܒܝܢܟ܁ ܐܝܟܢܐ ܕܒܫܡܝܐ ܐܦ ܒܐܪܥܐ܁ ܗܒ ܠܢ ܠܚܡܐ ܕܣܘܢܩܢܢ
ܝܘܡܢܐ܁ ܘܫܒܘܩ ܠܢ ܚܘܒܝܢ ܘܚܛܗܝܢ܁ ܐܝܟܢܐ ܕܐܦ ܚܢܢ ܫܒܩܢ
ܠܚܝܒܝܢ܁ ܘܠܐ ܬܥܠܢ ܠܢܣܝܘܢܐ܁ ܐܠܐ ܦܨܢ ܡܢ ܒܝܫܐ܁ ܡܛܠ
ܕܕܝܠܟ ܗܝ ܡܠܟܘܬܐ܁ ܘܚܝܠܐ ܘܬܫܒܘܚܬܐ ܠܥܠܡ ܥܠܡܝܢ܁

The Lord's Prayer in Common writing in Classical Aramaic

ܐܒܘܢ ܕܒܫܡܝܐ܁ ܢܬܩܕܫ ܫܡܟ܁ ܬܐܬܐ ܡܠܟܘܬܟ܁ ܢܗܘܐ ܨܒܝܢܟ܁ ܐܝܟܢܐ
ܕܒܫܡܝܐ ܐܦ ܒܐܪܥܐ܁ ܗܒ ܠܢ ܠܚܡܐ ܕܣܘܢܩܢܢ ܝܘܡܢܐ ܘܫܒܘܩ ܠܢ
ܚܘܒܝܢ ܘܚܛܗܝܢ܁ ܐܝܟܢܐ ܕܐܦ ܚܢܢ ܫܒܩܢ ܠܚܝܒܝܢ܁ ܘܠܐ ܬܥܠܢ
ܠܢܣܝܘܢܐ܁ ܐܠܐ ܦܨܢ ܡܢ ܒܝܫܐ܁ ܡܛܠ ܕܕܝܠܟ ܗܝ ܡܠܟܘܬܐ܁ ܘܚܝܠܐ
ܘܬܫܒܘܚܬܐ ܠܥܠܡ ܥܠܡܝܢ܁

The Lord's Prayer in Common Writing
in Modern Aramaic–Chaldean

ܒܒܢ ܕܐܝܠܗ ܒܫܡܝܐ܁ ܩܝܡ ܡܩܘܕܫܐ ܫܡܘܟ܁ ܐܬܝܐ ܡܠܟܘܬܘܟ܁ ܗܘܐ
ܨܒܝܢܘܟ܁ ܕܐܝܟ ܕܒܝܠܗ ܒܫܡܝܐ ܐܦܐܝܟ ܗܡ ܒܐܪܥܐ܁ ܗܒܠ ܠܣܢܐ ܕܣܘܢܩܢܢ
ܝܘܡܐ܁ ܘܫܒܘܩ ܛܠܒ ܠܚܬܢ ܘܚܛܝܬܢ܁ ܕܐܝܟ ܕܗܡ ܐܚܢܝ ܒܣܡܢ ܥܒܝܕܝ
ܕܡܣܟܘܕܝܠܢ ܐܝܠ܁ ܘܠܐ ܡܥܒܪܬܢ ܬܟܘܕܗ ܐܝܟ ܡܢܣܝܟܝܠ ܒ ܒܝܫܐ܁ ܡܛܠ
ܕܕܝܠܟܘܗ ܒܝܠܗ ܡܠܟܘܬܐ܁ ܘܚܝܠܐ ܘܬܫܒܘܚܬܐ ܠܥܠܡ ܥܠܡܝܢ܁

About the Author

Fr. Michael J. Bazzi

The Rev. Emeritus Fr. Michael J. Bazzi, L.S.T., has pastored at St. Peter Chaldean Catholic Church in El Cajon, San Diego, since 1985. Fr. Michael was also a professor of modern and classical Aramaic at Cuyamaca College in El Cajon. Fr. Michael is a distinguished Bible authority, author, teacher, linguist, translator, and pastoral counselor.

Born in Tilkepe, Iraq, a suburb of Nineveh, he graduated seminary at St. Peter's College, Baghdad, and was ordained into the priesthood in that same year, 1964. He served eight years in Tilkepe as an assisting priest, speaking his native language of Aramaic, as well as Arabic. He then travelled to the Vatican in Rome where he earned a Masters Degree in Pastoral Theology. While in Italy he gained a broad knowledge of the Italian and French languages.

Fr. Michael arrived in Oshkosh — Green Bay, Wisconsin in 1974. Here he taught and preached Scripture from the Aramaic point of view. Later, he established parishes in Oak Park and Troy, Michigan, and in 1983-85, served in Los Angeles, CA. Fr. Michael moved to San Diego in 1985. In 1987, he became pastor of St. Peters Church in El Cajon, where he is presently serving.

Fr. Michael was the San Diego Law Enforcement Associations' Citizen of the Year in 2010.